# ANCIENT SUNLIGHT

Stephen Watts

# ANCIENT SUNLIGHT

ENITHARMON PRESS

First published in 2014
by Enitharmon Press
10 Bury Place
London WC1A 2JL

www.enitharmon.co.uk

Distributed in the UK by
Central Books
99 Wallis Road
London E9 5LN

ISBN: 978-1-907587-29-0

Enitharmon Press gratefully acknowledges the financial support of
Arts Council England through Grants for the Arts.

British Library Cataloguing-in-Publication Data.
A catalogue record for this book is available
from the British Library.

Stephen Watts would like to thank Arts Council England for
support at various stages of the writing of these poems,
and Chris Gutkind for immense help in editing them.
With thanks also to Cristina Viti, Gareth Evans
and Marius Kociejowski for their support.

Designed in Albertina by Libanus Press
and printed in England by
SRP

# CONTENTS

*for Cristina*

I

# MÁIRTÍN Ó DIREÁIN

Máirtín, I walked to your home
   from the ferry pier at Cill Rónáin : it
was a lovely five miles, though it took me
fifty years. But it was a beautiful walking,
wild garlic on your paths, cormorant seas,
honeysuckle, furling bracken, honey bees.
I blew you a kiss when I got to your house
though you might not have wanted a kiss.
The little stream shimmied down the shore.
Below your barn bare limestone then more,
your stone path with tiny lilies going down.
A rain cloud is gathered across the spine of
your island where the houses climb the hill
above Corrúch where I walked into silence
and spoke with horses and lay down asleep
in all of those fourteen thousand little fields
each with its waterbed and drift of flowers.
It was quiet there. I heard silence swarming.
And liquid arrows bubbled inside my eyes :
yellow and molten, red and violet and blue.
Soon I will have to go, walking fast to reach
the five o'clock ferry back to Ros an Mhíl.
And then the bus to Galway and that banal,
savage bird, Shannon to Stansted. Not that
I wanted to, Máirtín : I'd rather stay here.
I eased my body under an upturned coracle
its blue-tarred carcass, then the sky above.
Now it's time to leave your house, I'll blow
you one more kiss, although you might not
want my kiss : this is what I came here for,
these words, the stone sleepers, language
that matters, language that can say "yes".
And the swell of real time against shores
      of inhabited space.

# BUT NOW I LIVE ON A SORROWFUL PLANET

*But now I live on a sorrowful planet*
Frida Kahlo

I should have worked as a porter in a remote hotel
or at the night-desk of a dour metropolitan hospital
I should have driven lorries before dawn down the
arteries of a weeping city
I should have handled tube trains into stations like
squealing pigs
I should have worked in a laundry or navvied it as
the foreman of a brickies' troupe,
I should have been a laughter-clown or trapezed my
life up your wide sistering streets.
Ah, but for now I just live on a sorrowful planet !
I should have got up before dawn and gone to the
mosque, to the women's entrance,
being a woman,
I should have portered in hospitals or given singing
lessons in oncology,
I should have run backwards up moorland meadows
and gone raving over the blackberry
hill,
I should have closed my eyes in the face of oncoming
tides, in the face of the patinas of
'no',
I should have tautened my nerves on the rage of
exhausted ligaments,
I should have belly-danced under g-nomes or taken
the cholesterol count of stem cells.
I should have looked at myself in the eyes of a monkey,
in the eyes of a dog,
I should have tied yellow ribbons on walnut branches,

I should have let myself collapse in the apricot valleys
of the highest sierras –
Ah, but I did none of these things, I painted the sun
as source of all energies, the rampant goddess
as swirl of life, the dog of my dreams,
the snake of all breath …

My grandfather worked in Pizza Express in Greek
Street in 1904

Except it wasn't Pizza Express then, it was Crameri
& Caruso's Italian Coffee Parlour

And my grandfather was second-head waiter and my

Mother was not far off being born in Phoenix Street in
the tenements opposite the theatre, the tenements
that were there until the seventies, until that is

They were pulled down & something else was put up
in their place, because it was regeneration time

And there's a photograph of her peeping round from
behind the ice-cream vendor's barrow as
if she knew what was to come

And every Sunday she'd go with her mother & father
to the red church in Soho Square

The church where a piece of cornice fell off & clipped
the biretta of a passing priest, o that priest
will pass by there no more,

And every Thursday for years after they'd moved to
the Creamery out in West Croydon – the one
in the arcade opposite the station

Every Thursday my grandfather'd take his daughter,
my mother, back into Soho to get the gossip,
the fresh pasta & spinach

And they'd sit in Lui Crameri's, he talking dialect with
his cronies, she squashed stiff into a windowless
corner unable to squeak

That same year Stalin & Lenin were over-nighting it
in Tower House in Fieldgate Street over here
for the 3rd International

And the Italian anarchists of Dean St. & Clerkenwell
glistened as they waited under the dewy moon
with greased daggers drawn

Hoping with surety that what would happen could be
swayed and vectored out of sync so that their
century might not have been

What, of course, it had to be. But no : it couldn't, it
couldn't, it simply couldn't be !

My grandfather painted ceilings somewhere in Soho,
bright with mountains in the sunlit snow &
virgin spirits in their peacock shrines !

And I stand here now in Fieldgate Street watching as
a corner of zinc flies from the coppice roof to
land by my unflummoxed feet

And I take the found zinc object as a door-stop for my
hearthless home – we who have to live in some
new degenerate regeneration zone

And as I eat my *fiorentina* in Frith Street I remember
all of this, and all I can say to the waitress who's
asking 'Would I like another coffee yet'

Is 'what is the number of this century we are living in'
    & 'how did we get to where duplicity is become
        the ordinary nature of our breath ?'

& 'political hurt can hurt us no more' & 'the noise of
    the heart is a furtive claw' & 'the remote places
        are the heart of our world'

& 'the colours of blood are war-flags unfurled' & 'the
    war against terror is an error of fear' & 'all
        of us shimmie toward ordinary death'

Then I paid & rushed out penniless into the peacock-
    shrieking street, flummoxed to know I'd
        met exactly who I'd had to meet.

## CHESHIRE STREET

Among all the rakers of Cheshire Street, among
　　　　　traders in bananas & apples
off tressel-tables on street corners, among dealers in
Doc Martens and plimsolls under mild autumn suns,
among villains & wreckers & backyarded emperors,
　　　　　where the neurotic bookseller used
to deal in toxins and leather, where you could barter
old negatives for a coin or a kiss, where you might be
able to find postcards of your grandmother or pastels
　　　　　of some orange grove,
or photographs of banditeering Kurds from Saqqez,
under the mild sun where you could remember snow,
under a mild sun where you could not predict 'now',
　　　　　under the mild sun in
your own unpredictable mildness, attacking no-one !
In Blackman's bootshop, in Majer's street of dreams,
　　　　　in the kingdom of Charlie Burns,
in the market where John Sheehy came after leading
his donkey over from Ealing on the epic journey that
　　　　　lasted four & forty years & many pubs :
　　　　　I ask you ! I am telling you !
　　　　　Now ! …
Among the rare rakers & pullers of Cheshire Street.
　　　　　Along with Alan Dein in
the mild October sun, along with Rachel Lichtenstein.
In the traumas of memory & the little nauseas of time
where old bombs fell and new bombs will be hatched.
In those most mild of airs, those most soporific suns !
　　　　　Suddenly I plunge south into
the river of dreams and lean into the cave of memory,
and contort myself through unmanageable portals,
　　　　　through the space that isn't there,
　　　　　but is ! And then after

decades suffered in the reflexes of tar, I rise gasping
through the bubbles of the deep stream : and look ! –
Cheshire Street is gone,
the bridge of dreams is gone, Majer & the market are
gone, the mountains of blood are gone, the donkeys of
memory are gone, the body in the glacier is gone,
our bodies that go,
are gone !
And rising through bubbles of deep time I can see :
blank faces with blunt eyes in shaman-trance,
skin-peeling back the dancer
from the dance

## LISTENING TO DINU LIPATTI PLAY BACH

I am sitting here listening to Dinu Lipatti playing
Bach, while outside
the evening is going
to grey

I am sitting here, listening in amazement because
a cold girl stands furious in the
middle air
and single notes float
out beyond the place where they should stop
or where they should become
so remote

that all sound would cease, but look : there
is no end to breathing – or no
peace

unless a shudder of the earth, its crust already betrayed by
unlinked, furtive magmas were
to explode on

some surface of our soils
once more

tearing trees from roots and brown veins,
placing rock shards high into
cold air

But I am sitting here listening to Dinu Lipatti play chorales and
partitas of Bach : & all else is illusion
or else a new explosion

## A LITTLE MESSAGE TO MY FRIEND RUMI

I am writing you this because I don't want to lose
my sanity.

I am writing you this because I want to be insane.

Everything amounts to the same. There is no best
or better answer. All of language
is a disadvantage.

In the autumn I'll go to live on an island near Brac
to work on translations with my dear
and Hvar friends :

It all amounts to the same : language and the sun.

The red mountain has melted in my blood. The red
mountain is covered with weeds of mist :

If you place your foot on the peat-bogs of bounce
you will echo back from the hearths
of deep rock below :

And where the shark-toothed mountains rise : old
trawlers came in to the havens by
the skerries at night :

Their starboard lanterns swayed the laws of time.

What does death mean, or the loss of language ? Or
stones flung by women against sisters who
have gone against the dictates of
sour mullahs ?

I knew a man wrote poems to the birds in the trees
and sat amidst drunkards and spat with
them, spat words of

Delirium and joy and harshness and blind decoy :
for what else would matter to tart
wings of delirium ?

He was a walking archive of the communed tongue.
He was not destroyed by the world
with which he fell in
love !

Hah !

He was clever, that one, not to be entranced : I know
a mountain set above an alpine hut –

I know I should sleep
on the floor by your foot : nothing
is left : only dust &

the aching penumbra of my
breath.

## WATNEY MARKET, OCTOBER 2006

We're all nomads really, in a nomad world.

Those of us who stand in the market-place &
        scratch our heads.

Those of us whose fathers were born in Sylhet.

Those of us whose mothers are called Begum
        or Miah or Longhi

How did we get up this morning in our daze?

How did we manage that imperfect feat of our
        most disingenuous balance?

And how did we carry ourselves to this point in
        space and time, in the market of
        our days?

Bearing in mind neither space nor time actually
        exist.

Look! A bicycle plunges down the slope of dreams.

And next a baby so alert, propelled by his mother
        in her lamenting exhaustion.

Look how the metal flags don't flutter in the wind.

Look at the cabbages, aubergines, lemons, pears.

Look at the orange peppers and okra, the plantains
        and sweet potatoes, the flat-fish and
        neuroses

Look at the bolts of cloth, the carpets, the bread !

None of it exists ! Neither the chadored girl who
      screamed in her loving last night

Nor the tower block she has just emerged from to
      fetch her shopping back home

The shopping that'll feed her family up the tower
      block, collapsed by the corporation
      all those years ago.

## LITTLE FICTION FOR LOVELY NICHITA
### STĂNESCU

The sun has risen & burnt a hole in the gauze
of the skies and now
a full moon is swimming in the quiet horizons.
Little ice paths spangle the obdurate tilth of
your slippery fields


Nichita, I recall seeing you crossing the village
street, led through the vodka ruts
by your neighbour's son – you dressed in that
outsize pullover that is almost definitive of
poetry in an autistic age


I think you never walked to Paris or rolled over
the Ardennes on
your Harley Davidson : maybe you did, but if so
you didn't ever tell me. I think you stayed on in
villages of deluged rage


Nichita, how is it possible so much time's gone by
when so few years have elapsed ?
What's this ambiguous life that we've lived our
unrest through ? What held still in the jasmine
of your eyes ?

Under a caustic moonlight, in an air of tangerine
                    suns. Can't you see amidst all
this wreckage, our cravings for human freedoms ?
Our freedoms that are kin to voluntary poverty,
                    as Vladimír Holan reasoned …


It is too long since you were with us, though I know
                    you never left. Even so
in these years lacking alchemy & language all of us
feel bereft, feel we need the conjure of your poetry,
                    your verve, its jest

## EARLY MORNING VISIT FROM
## DAVID SILVER

David Silver came round again today
Early, after a gap of five or six years

His Irish woman from Coventry's gone
He's back on the fags but off the booze

And saved a thousand pounds & more
& lost nine hundred papering his door

He's still at 50 Dominie Road, Bow E3
Two televisions (one big, one small), a

Table, settee-set, fridge, no washing
Machine, cooker (but he never cooks),

Meals-On-Wheels on seven day-tickets,
A giro weekly & monthly though quite

Why he's never really known. A Social
Worker calls in on Tuesday every week

She's Finnish & good, with trousers, he
Says : like a beatnik with a leather coat.

Kind heart and head, and hands to help
Fill out his forms & tell him to stay still.

David's got a kitchen, bedroom, a hall,
Bathroom and as he says a living room

A double-bed though he's always alone,
A sink, a tap, a radio-video, a telephone,

One joey-budgie, no longer cat or dog :
The ginger latter run over, some catter

Got the cat, or else it just went its way.
Who in this life anyway is here to stay ?

His goldfish jumped out from its bowl
And fell between a dustpan and a stool

His mum & dad are long gone & dead
One brother married, he's pretty sure :

He went to the wedding. Not seen any
Brother or sister in about twenty year.

One of them's a ginger beard, glasses.
The other lost his wages on the horses.

He asks me for a letter with its stamp
Part so he can copy down my address

Part because he likes the yellow shape
And part so he can get a friend or his

Finnish social worker to write out what
He wants to say to me : David himself

Can neither read nor write : a dunce
He says but I say no dunce just badly

Taught, never put back from truancy
Or ever schooled for unskilled living.

What is a truant in this ordered life, if
Not a beggar-man or poor giving-thief?

He asks me is he fifty-nine or sixty yet:
Born March 20th 1944: I say fifty-nine

But add he is whatever he wants to be,
He's free to choose, to be or not to, but

In the glut of a queue, of course he's not.
Freedom's just a token given to the few.

He says his neighbours are all cheats &
Robbers, some chickling aimed a rocket

Through his door-flap last Guy Fawkes
Night that burnt down bed and bedroom

And put him out of house but now he's
Back and in the daily rhythm of his lack

He wants to take my bust alarm-clock
With large numbers printed on its face

He wants me to be his pen-friend since
He hardly ever comes to Shadwell now

He gives me fifty p because he couldn't
Give me any for my birthday or a card

And says his Social Worker's told him
About classes in music, cars & cooking

At One-Stop Shops and old Town Halls
Or learning how to read & how to write.

He's lit up a fag and I've said that's fine
Though I don't like smokes in my home

And I've not wanted this poem to rhyme
Though it could but what'd be the point

It's not as if our lives have such order :
I've a fiver in my pocket (plus fifty p !)

And no knowing when the next is due :
I don't care whether I eat or sleep at all

Or if anyone reads this poem any more.
I write it as it makes me happy in time

Of war. Anyone with any sense can hear
An inner rhythm ticking against my fear.

Next month I'm going to Galway to read.
Maybe that's where David's lady's gone

But I'll not see her there I'm pretty sure.
David himself likes pure history books &

Takes the picture ones from his library :
A lending van on wheels but its blue door

Opens him shut with knowledge and puts
A dunce's cap on every time it takes it off

He's stopped drinking now but buys all
His food and juice from an Offie close-by

His home in Bow. Bow : Bow of the Bells
Bow of the Match Girls, Bow of the Cows

That once got milked up tin churn alleys.
Bow of the Quadrants, Bow of the Attics,

Rich Bow, Poor Bow, Beggar Bow, Thief.
Bow ... Bo ... Bah ... Beh ... Blah ... Baah.

When he leaves my home (he had been up
The London for a blood-test that was why

He'd come this way) having found me here,
Turns to wave as I stand at my open door

And I'll wait for the first card/letter from
The first pen-friend I've had since I was 8

"Sorry I can't always come round to visit,
I will try to send you a birthday card next

Week : I get a month's money about then.
I'm going to get myself a washing machine

Or try to. I could send you a clothes parcel
If you are short of trousers. A friend at 48

Is writing this for me. I've got to go & buy
A stamp album to start saving stamps. I'll

Send this from 50 Dominie Road, E3 4EN
& bless you, David S., your true old friend."

And then he adds but doesn't know if I will
Get off at Mile End then find the Cemetery.

Ask for Dominie Road & just cut through.
Come with a stick but be not blind. I'll try.

I've chimed this poem on the years he's had
I'm not bothered with rhyme but – so what

I've written this just for what David's got …

# FOR MY FRIEND, MAX SEBALD

*Tell them I had a wonderful life*
Ludwig Wittgenstein


Two months ago I was
talking to you in the Lithuanian forests : telling you
how old women from out of Druskininkai were walking
the blue floors of those stretched oceans with buckets
of mushrooms and moss


There space is old, trees are tall, memory is pain,
history is full of partisans and a sufi music conjures all
of us to whirl where the stalks of the forest barely sway.
I sensed you there because of the rotting of the music
and I knew you'd care.


Your room still is full of photographs
your realm looked after by trees. You who eschewed all
computer trails have been taken away by a skidding wheel
by black ice or a seizure of the heart, lifelong discourse
and your daughter's hurt


All I can do now is stagger
round my rooms mewling out your name Max, Max :
what will happen to language now, now you are not here
and who is left and how many remain of the anarchists
on the ice-floes of speech

These last weeks I had been
writing you postcards in my head : Max come to Whitechapel.
Come soon. Come and talk. Come and walk. Where are you ?
Why did you ? : but this has become an explosion of words
on the scarp of my pain


We'd talked about walking
from my village to yours : cutting a section across the Alps
or a section through a glacier's brain. From Precasaglio
in the Alta Valcamonica to Wertach in the Allgäu.
Now I will do that without you.


Before we met and surely ever since
we've been talking to each other. And even when the other
was not there we'd carry on in monologues to hear. I shall
go on talking to you for as long as my mouth can speak :
or what is the point of language


From where did I come
to this scarred field : you first heard my voice in your car,
you last lost your own voice there : what silence in the water,
what bird-smoke, what rough circle in our language has
brought us back to here ?


Dear friend, what is the use of speech :
I now asking of you questions you can no longer reach –
yet as you drift off to the snow-hole of your hills I hear
you say "they are ever returning to us, the dead" –
Max, I am listening …

# TIME : ITS RHAPSODY

There is a point in time

just after nightfall with the western sky
                        on pale black
and close by the inter-city railhead with its
                                    tannoys


There is a point in time

far from mother or father or love or anything

when a raw man on crutches and without
                        the power of money
is trying to negotiate the way beyond all mess
        to get to St. Mungo's refuge
                or to sanctuary


There is a point in time when both in all logic
                        and from all love
we should wonder not why this earth was
                                    created


but why we ourselves have made it as it is :


And where the white cranes rise like heron
            in wait over the stream of cars
and when the works are complete and then
            the travel of trains is begun

and when the slow murmur of machinery is
                    not memory-pulsed in
                              our breathing
and when spotlights search out our places
                              of sleep ...


There is a time in every city
when constant love fails, when communities
                              collapse
when asylum is barred and wars are declared
                    only for the sake of politics
when all love fails and yet life goes on but
          not the life and the love
                    we really need
and betrayal is in the breath of all rulers and
                    betrayal is become breath
          and, worse still, breath itself has
                    become betrayal :


Then, tell me a few words of sanity from your
                    city :
          there is not much left to say, anyway,
                    is there !

But tell me a few bare words of sanity from
                    where you are :

Tell me how suffering has driven enough of
                    us out of our minds
          and others to an insane pursuit
                    of premature sanity.

Tell me it is blunt cynicisms have done such
things to us :

That there is a point in time when there is no
point in time at all

There is a point in time where lucid language
becomes a betrayal

There is a point in time when time's shattered,
when it ceases to be, ceases to be time and
when fractured time moves
us only to abuse
each other


I say this to you, little one, because all of us
are small, and being small we
can see the detail …


I say all of this to you, even though listening
ceased many years ago, because all
of us with out exception are
huge

So huge that we can see the whole expanse,
glittering on its ludic hill


I say this in place of watching television or
seeing newspapers

I say this instead of being glutted with fat
images in a maggot-city


As might pull us out of death with time


But time cannot so easily be destroyed

I say this in spite of the violence of our
ambition and spite

I say this because, truly, there are no
more words left to say

# ANA META BRAMSCI

I know a very lovely woman,
       a dear friend if ever
          there is one :

Her name – why shouldn't I tell you all – is

            Ana-Meta-Bramsi

     Except that sometimes she changes it a little
       and then she may become for
         a while Meta Ana
         Vramsi

         Bah ! Porque no ?

     (bah ! there is method in her madness !)

For this Ana Meta-Meta Ana has without doubt
      the abilities to metamorphose, to shape-change or
        change the shape of things, to
            translate one world into
              another …

Sometimes she lives in Trnovo, sometimes Trzin, some-
    times she inhabits her own zone, sometimes
        she goes Hvar away

    Sometimes she goes wireless in Maribor, some
      times she sleeps at the sea shore,
        just now she's away

in Santiniketan …


Her favourite poet may be WBY or Rabindranath
Tagore, but then just as easily that one –
without the least taste of
infidelity –


might be Gregor Strniša, or Marina
Tsvetaeva, or even
(pardon her taste) crack-headed
Stevek

Or better still, Mister Today 4-ever !


O Iztok Osojnik !

O happy-slappy Srečko


( ! tick-
tack//
tock-
tick !)


She's many ages at once is Meta Ana : somewhere just
past fifty, somewhere nearish to thirty,
something like fifteen

she wanders – like we all do – between
seven and seventy, between
nought & ninety

Sometimes she loves listening to Nusrat Ali Fateh – or
if she khan't then Bach (no, no Bramsi just
you stay calm) or Mikís Theodolitis
(or maybe I have his name
wrong ?) :

or maybe to Nick Cave or to Nick Drake

( ! tick-tack//tock-tick !)


Or if no music is to be found, then the lucid sounds of
Jose Pletnikar plucking on the distinction
between homo and ludens

(so bloody European !)


And sometimes she just does nothing, being an expert
at that most vital art, replenishing air

swimming in the sea, dreaming
cormorants off the coasts
of Hvar,

until she again can breathe, as we, her friends,
would want her to

as we do, as & when & if we can,
since breath
gives all of us freedom

&

freedom replenishes

breath

and laughter

gifts us life

&

so

let's live !

II

# BIRDS OF EAST LONDON

When you live on the twenty-first floor of a tower
and way past midnight you hear a fracture
of wings and in the morning there's
a collar-dove on your balcony

is that a dream ?

When you live on the twenty-first floor and you get
home just at dawn from a party – or you've
been working at the desk all night, the
desk of words I mean – and the
mist you've travelled
home through

lies

flannelled just beneath
your feet so you cannot see the
ground and yet the whole
sky is king-fissure
blue

from the palest horizon to the most golden baroque

is that also a dream
but is it not also
the most real … ?

And out of such skies come birds and bombs …


When you live on the twenty-first floor and you
notice that in a crack in the cladding
a few metres down a kestrel
has made her nest


and when you see that kestrel
pinioned on its wing-bone, sitting at ease in
the middle air, shifting sideways on sudden
gusts – its unperplexed ligaments
ready to dive it through
skies of reality


through torn webs of nerves


and when you catch
the feather of the collar-dove
floating past your eye …


is that not a dream and
is life only a dream ?


Or when you see Arctic geese flying beneath your feet
toward the landing stage on the Camargue just
as once you saw them flying


between the mountain and the sea – in
the gap between sight and nothing
right there above your head –
on those far islands of
mica schist

way out west and beyond
the times of
clearance


is that only a dream or does life
just dream us ?


And language has broken down, language has been
bandaged – like the sun, like the bandaged
sun – and we speak in chunks
of betrayal words

when language itself
has become …


Or when at eye level from your balcony you see black
darting swifts mewing in the fine drizzle or
turning their sleek bodies in the
sun as they bite tiny insects
imply for sustenance


is this just a dream of
life ?


Or the gannet that plunges down cliffs of light
(as a broke lift might through shafts of
darkness) and breaks the surface
of the curdled water leaving
its tongue's graffiti on
the shoal beneath

having picked out just one fish
for its gizzard and gullet


O my toppled sanity : O my maytime
market : O my bridge of
dreams


Or as a cormorant might
fly straight into the sun
and either it will crinkle and fizz in the black
heats – or else it will heal the sun's
bandaged
wound :


(for this is what birds know that we
no longer know)


Or the stormy petrel sleeping on the heave of
the ocean, giving countenance to
the wreck and the wrack
waiting for the spigot or flag
of seaweed or the onrush of
maritime tide


One time in my house on the burnt island a wren
deep-dived by a buzzard fled in through
my blue open door but then was as
bone burst by human space
as by any beak or claw

though I spoke to it
in bird words from the piece of
my hearth

and I cupped it in my hands
until off it flew

but my mind is a burnt island : as is
everyone's in this bruised
world, or in this world
of bruised minds

and is everyone just a
dream ?


When you live on the twenty-first floor and the old
Ukrainian man twelve floors down keeps
racing pigeons on his balcony –
Popa he is called
and he sings
lullabies
in

the sunlit pub on Cable Street
the pub that is not yet
shut down –

and

his pigeons fly in wide arcs, in circles
from his balcony, but they cannot
return him to the village
near Lv'ov (shhh
shhh :

this is his mother hugging him close
shielding his eyes, clasping him
to her body lest he moan
or whimper when
the partisans
piss in

the bushes she's hiding him in as
they pass through the
burnt village :

shhh .. shhh)


Is this then just a dream ?


Or when you live on the twenty-first floor and
you see two cormorants sweeping the sky
making wide arcs of their own choice
bargaining with no-one and
compromising nothing :


what in their bone structure
do they know that we will never
know ?


what in the balance between
their gut and their eye ?


and suddenly from sweeping the city they
streak and scud from one

sector of the city to
another

from one skerry to the
burning sun

(corporations named cars after animals, governments
named bombs after birds)

even language has its final answer, even
words fail – or else soar –
where we most need them

even birds fly in East London
coming from Iceland or the Western Isles
going to Morocco or Algeria or
south of the Sahara …

Is this just a dream ?
this
parliament of birds, these
migrations

this flight path of swifts and swallows
this discourse on the sanities
this journey to be made
across breath

or

the stupidity of ever drawing
boundaries


When you live on the twenty-first floor and down
there in the paved market you can see
your friends ...

# OLD WOMEN OF MY CHILDHOODS

Everytime I walk
Into an alley plunged in black sunlight
I remember old women from my childhoods

Their long dresses
Their crêpe skin that amazed me
The tiny flowers in the bowl of their faces
The black shawls when they worked
Their meadows, their fields and gardens
Silence that contained only answers of
Those old women plunged in sunlight

And from my first childhood
And circle of sunlight in the flower garden
And the daisies grown higher than my head
And my mouth that went through the fence
To kiss the mouth of the curly girl next door
And the magnified grasses when I lay
My face on the earth's soil

   And in my next childhood
And the one that came after my first
And was consumed with isolation and with
          the insane pursuit of premature
                    sanity

The one I spent schooled in order
that torn childhood when line and colour
were forcibly parted from language

In this new and easily come-by childhood
Every time I walked through an alleyway
held tight in the drizzles of soft rain

Every time this happened I
remembered the old women of
                my childhoods


My aunt from
the city of china and canals
pottering in her goods yard
craving snowdrops from coal
kettles from coal-dust

Look !
She's bringing out the tin
bath to sud out all her bulges :

She who played
cricket with me in the garden
and read me bed-time stories


My grandmother in her long dress
Standing in the sun of another country
Standing in the militancy of her mildness

Standing like an alley plunged in light
A route to the future and not the past
In her lucid disregard for good sense


And my mother who
By the time of my third childhood
Had entered the last years of her own
And already herself was old

My mother then
I thought of almost as a child
Shopping for fresh pasta and winter coats
With her father in the shops of Frith
                              Street

And in those years
I carried her once in my arms
Up steep meadows to the mountain hut
And cooked for her as she for years
Had done the same but more
                    for me


And in my third childhood
the one that comes before the fourth
the one that is predicated on all the sanities
                              of madness
on all that is disreputable and indissoluble
& protests and proteins timed on youth


And in my final childhood
And that of the insanity I have yet to attain
Whenever I hobble into alleys of sunlight
And whenever I walk through walls
Through their non-existent holes
Into the drivel of words and
            the palaver of farewells


I remember the old women
Of my childhoods and my early years
And of all the years I have put together
Shattered in alleys & plunged in black light

And when I dribble my goodbyes
And when I forget the arts of parting
I think back on my grandmother
Held between nutmeg and mountain birds
Held between polenta and a fistful of cloves
Held just where history exploded her

And in the later years
Those when the afterbirths of childhood
Had been thrown aside and not wrapped round
To heal memory or poultice political wound …

And when the line of white on
My unshaven face is like a brittle field
Of hoar-frost with pecking birds

In those later years
I want to think back on the lives of
old women I have known …

My grandmother
standing amazed and certain in her
superb seventeen years beauty

My grandmother standing
out of sepia with her eldest children
dressed in white for the camera
my mother also standing and
looking out through thick thin
turbulents of brown time

My grandmother
Leaning on her leaning stick

On the arm of my aunt
The amazed compassion of her youth
Still smiling from out her face ...


Is that what is meant by migration ?


A smile moving from one face to another ...

My grandmother
Was an economic migrant in time of war
Losing two babies at the border post
To the fiction of disease and
Unnecessary papers


Is that what is meant by asylum ?

I also with my words plunder matter :

Am I then master of what matters ?


Or old women
I knew in the Western Isles
Who never in their lives left their island
Nor even one township of it nor
Hardly even a hearth

But for summer pasture on the shieling moors ...

Or to handle herring on other eastern shores
Fingers cold-charred with gluey fish-scales ...

And yet the candour of their mouths
And yet the clamour of their justice …


Or in my next childhood
And in my last but one when I had learnt
To count by a different system through this life
Through this stubborn uninhibiting uninhabitable
                                festering of breaking things


When even breath had become a betrayal
And language was a midden-heap of maggots
                                and worms


Or in the final childhood I will never attain
When we come to realise all the beautiful insanities
                                of compassion

And I managed fully to lose my sanity
Only whilst fully managing to retain it

And in this way I was able to walk again
Into the dark alleys of black sunlight

And to remember the old women of my childhoods

And therefore to crease out the lines of my life

And the palpable imbecility of ever drawing
                                boundaries

## BRICK LANE MELA POEM

Ghosts come pouring out the houses
words have clogged
my throat : this mild winter I'll put
on my mountain scarf and go out in
the dark :


I'll slowly walk down the slight curve
and incline of the Lane,
my hand in the hands of my friends in
a tight drizzle towards the fizz of far
light


Toward the tunnel of dark air that
is neither light nor real,
but either must be Bethnal Green or
else is Beani Bazar or the relic of a
curling dream


And as I walk I am talking to ghosts
and they are
my friends and they answer with mild
herbs of speech to calm me, as surely
as I shamble


Past the oast-houses and mud fields of
Shuttle Street
and even as I curve back on Woodseer
a tinsmith is hammering cups next
to Banglatown C&C

And a man is pushing a trolley through
                    Sylhet Town
and I'm become as old and young as I am
and I float in curved space in the black
                    light of this lane


Here is Kafka's Dora who opened a café
                    with her brother
at 53 Brick Lane after the war. Here's
the string shop intact with its window
                    nailed to the moon


And my friend Nazrul Islam, the one
                    who wrote *Vidrohi*
on the back of his hand. I am talking
to ghosts as I talk to my friends and
                    here in her car


Comes Shamim Azad, just in time as I
                    treat myself to a bowl of dhall :
join me dear friend, help coax lemon in
the lentil or fold the curd and unbone
                    the ilish-fish


And here is Nazrul Naz buying papers
                    at the last Sangeeta
translating Obaidullah while the whole
vortex of Brick Lane rears up and curls
                    round on its circle

Bill Fishman walks due south talking
                    to his dead dad,
Majer Bogdanski plays his violin stood
in the middle of the Lane and no-one
                    wants to complain


I walk out in the dark light of the road
                    & hear the rotting of a sufi music
and I fall apart – or how else would I find
the mad-rapt sound I need and nowhere
                    else can find


Let me hear music or I will not go mad
                    and I want to lose
this sense and arthritis and spinning tin
of rationed time that ends and begins
                    just where the Lane


Disappears : let me loose all sense or I'll
                    not see what's looming
at the edge or hear the singers in the Mela
or taste the clay-baked fish and lassis of
                    this swimming street


Raw musics burst in my head and make
                    stilt paths for my feet
as I shamble histories on this rooted coil
and seek the ever-precious venoms of
                    the curly snake

David Rodinsky walks by hand in hand
with Rachel
Lichtenstein : and Miriam Nelken rides
her drunken bike on toward the flower
meadows of her mind


Jeff Perks painted Brick Lane seamless
as a garment,
Avrom Stencl's sat beneath a thorn tree
talking to the birds and the drunk men
pelted with night's rind


Look at how they shine in the resident
air, yet no-one
sees them – because they are not there :
but I know they are & think of them
ghostly, ghostly


I see Dan Jones & Polly & Pola Uddin
outside Café Naz :
It was the cinema where anti-Nazis met.
Look : Tassaduq Ahmed has stopped
in the road to talk.


North of all time and of sound a lion cub
is nose-sniffed
by a hair-singed hound : and just around
the edge a singer staggers in amongst
hob-nailed boots

In the Knave Of Hearts market women
and men drink away
the cold, while outside street kids talk to
donkeys and invisible singing birds
perch on nothing's


Branch and in the Bar, men and women
lift glasses that are half-full
and Markéta Luskačová frames their lives
with pilgrims and holy wanderers from
the nomad world


Or by sleet-fires the aged young take
their tinnies and their tea,
burning cardboard on palettes of wood
because nobody else knows what it's
like to have stood


In the exact phases of their lives. Peace
to their blood, as
to their eyes : they are ghosts of whom
I speak, song-birds sit in their duffelled
hoods


And the Chicken Man of Leyden Street
car-washes
bloodied feathers from off his dungarees,
then ups and buys warmed beigels that
ooze cream-cheese

Up Sclater Street men as old as me gob
                on bacon butties
and from enamel cups off table tops –
like all of us have always done – drink
                pints of tea


Back in the mela-storm of the day I'll
                nip into the Meraj or
my Sweet & Spicy and write this poem
on dough-fresh chapatti in milli-script
                until it's done


And up above, the round filled moon is
                clay-baked bread,
as if Kolkota Sukanto had not died young
or beautiful Jibanananda was living still
                in Barisal


Then he'll take this world and place it in
                its turning clay or
microwave it till the darkening of the day
until it glints and pecks like songbirds
                in wet trees


Or when the city gets up off its knees
                to weep
and tower blocks shed their pastel skins
and walk beyond the herded city limits
                in sheets of sleet

I'll think back to this clay & sand and
                    brick-limned lane
back through ha'penny candle-lighters
and silk attics and weaver birds and
                    straw floors


And mulberry fruit and horse manure
                    and way-paths
winding through suburb fields, and mud
and more and the housing of the mad
                    & all of human betrayal


And wattle & pleasance & jugular woad
                    until I pull myself from
such streams to strudel from the all-night
baker's or burfi and jelabi from Ambala
                    & Alauddin


This street's become the river of our spate
                    and all of us are flowing :
all the living and the dead who congregate
eeling a way through life & maelstromed
                    outside doubt


As we walk along the middle of the lane,
                    all cars banished,
all traffic body, blood and unboned cloth
gone in the trick of music, or the magic
                    of the mela

Such fish we are here : slabbed carp with
blinded eyes, raw dog-fish,
stilt-walking fish and neon-ray-fish, deep-
mud fish and perch and pike, and then
a dream of hilsa


And here somewhere between midnight
and the dawn – in
the heat of it and nearly at its heart, all of
pain and succour and the bone mounted
beneath our skin


All the cream of it, all the ice-cold of it,
here where we stand and
raw history gushing us past on the river
of our street, not holding back coiling
waters of our spate

## MY MOTHER, HER TONGUE

When the body leaves the body with such
        suddenness, such speed,
when there is no time to draw a face, to say
a word, to hold a voice in memory – where
        are you gone ?


I went into your garden and walked on its
        brittle grass : the little
trees were stiff with frost and the sun drank
milk from the pewter of its glass, o mother
        white as jasmine


I cupped the shaman's cup in my hand &
        tossed it to and fro,
your body has become these rancid flowers
that in the night-time glow, but where now
        are you ?


Birds came to me in that garden – swallows
        turning their high bellies –
they spoke to my fingers with their tongues,
they filled the air, inside my head and out,
        but where are you ?


Car of death that moves off at the speed of
        the living,
car of death that moves off at walking pace,
unendured pain of peace, sun wrapped
        in its own linen

Wisteria and summer honeysuckle melted
their scents in that yard,
jasmine and lilac, basil and mint and apple,
grasses that were magnified beneath my
eye where I lay ...


Horses drifted into that garden way past
midnight : they nuzzled
the windows and the door. I saw their hoof
prints in the snow : what dream was that,
mother of jasmine


As a child I was happy in the garden of your
house : through
an air of daisies taller than my head to where
a tiny sun shone through the milky belly
of a horse


There was a litany, a bright effacement,
you were there who
were no longer there, seamstress-swallow
pulling needles of air through the cloth
of my sight


Little fish of the midday sun, little fish in
the air swimming,
little fish that gobbled oxygen and insects,
I see you turn high up over your wing
to look down at me

I see you fling the blue vocable 'never' with
its dull meaning against
the void of the sky where it explodes colour
in the space where nothing happens, o you
in the summer of jasmine


When your ashes were scattered you became
those flowers, you became
these trees, you became those birds that fling
their songs across torn webs of sky leaping
from goblets of light


You are not ashes, you are a tree unfurled
from where the soil and air
are slung against a silent wind that folds me
back from despair, o language coming from
you white as jasmine


You've flown between the frost and the sun,
you never were ash
in the charnel-house, the ordinary guards of
death had no meaning before the jasmine
of your face


Now your body is gone and your discourse,
your spirit like a bird is flown,
I strain to measure your voice in my lungs
but I know colliding rivers have loosed
my mother tongue

I was not there when the bird of your soul
       flew off from your body, I
could not watch that final trance and when
I was late come your breath was no longer
            making


Its slow unmeasured dance across the floor,
       when I got to your death your
mouth was already set in its trancing curve,
your nose was held and bent against those
         jasmines of your face


I do not know if it was the struggle with
       the oxygen mask (you
trying to push that sudden strangler off)
or if it was the struggle to stay alive that
         stopped your breath


This body, this light, these words, this work :
       where are you now ?
What dialect of the mother-tongue rose into
your mouth before being reeled back to this
         fading dream ?


You took that sense to where your ashes
       flock as dancing birds –
you singing across blueness to those snows
where shaman meditate the dying of
             their sisters

What shaman words can sing against my
           dullness now ?
What melted core of language has stunned
my mother-tongue ? That slow lark rising
                    from stiff snow


In its cliff-face field in mild January winds
           it's become the bird you,
weaving breath from under streamy cirrus
and the earth that seemed to stagger under
                    me as you flew


You were a spinning top in front of an
           open fire : I was
watching colour fly and we were talking
and what was dull was melted down to
                    this still measure


Car of death that moved at the speed of
           the living, car of death
that moved at a walking pace, unendured
pain of peace, sun that was wrapped in
                    its own linen


When I came back to the house I knew you
           were still there –
though much of the house was gone – and
I cried out through the world's war to you,
           O mother white as jasmine

The house is blind without you inside : but
        I am lifting it as
a lantern and swing it through its barriers
of pain and there is affirmation in this
            graft of light


The house is blind without your eyes, but
        you are still there,
wrapping pancakes in lemon, tired limbs
in warm sheets, folding pastry on apple,
            roasting meats


The house is blind without your eyes, but
        I will walk in your
door and rub my face stiff with frost and
bring roses inside that will flower in your
            tender house


And I will bring pasta and mushrooms and
        spinach and aniseed loaves,
this time I will bake bread and pour coffee
from a green jug to feed you, as once you
            fed me


I will bring milk and polenta and red wine,
        and mackerel with thyme,
sour-sweet apples from the garden, broccoli,
mint and burnt sugar : not enough, for all
            you gave

You who lived fifty years in the same house
                    what happened when
you passed over to the language of silence ?
What dialect of the mother-tongue faded
                    from your face ?


In your last years your skin became as crêpe
                    paper is
and who knows but it was you wrapped inside
thinking on your nieces and your nephews
                    and your sons


Your face has irrevocably changed : I will
                    wipe clear the white
walls of your house and you will rise in flight :
bird of jasmine, tree of frost, starling burst,
                    glint of schist


Swallows are dancing above the barn-half in
                    the slow trapeze of the sky,
stretched cirrus is carded in the weave of air :
how is it possible that memory can travel
                    back so far ?


Your own mother is calling back toward you
                    in the plum harvest,
along the vine terrace, into the cow-house,
across the snows of calm or in the valleys
                    of the mountain

You are still in the barn-half of that house
jumping from the threshold
down to steamy hay with milk-drunk calves
then running through the thick wood doors
out to jasmine air


Dun cows walk past the blunt end of a byre
and I can hear you hear
their belling necks then see their bellies sway
past as they veer out onto the pasture slope
into jasmine air


And the red mountain collapses and the red
mountain is still there,
and the red mountain is a road and is a river
and rises through my blood as melted mess
held there as love


Because the dead do not die when they die,
because the dead
always die when they die, because the shaman
of death is a bird in this translation of breath
into words


One time I carried you the last few metres to
the mountain hut. Now
your body is leaving you as you sleep and you
can see your waiting mother calling to you
from the slope

You remember your childhood dialects as
you die, their curt
abbreviations clinging close to breath, then
air lifts you and you look back at us from
jasmine night


And I write this in happy memory of you :
a song to be sung,
a flight of birds across a burning sky, bare
feet on wet grass, aniseed loaves looped on
poles to dry


And I write this poem to celebrate you :
words white as jasmine,
a sutra for when the body's left the soul,
a song to be sung for the life-line of the
mother-tongue

# PRAHA POEM

## *1

The high walls of Vojanovy Sady
Opposite the house of the poet Holan

Behind one the medieval cantata
And the may-time conference of the birds

And behind the other :
Centuries of silence, broken wings and
The dark pain of the moon child

What more can be said, little one :

Almost mathematically
That as much as once we loved

We now hate


## *2

As soon as I got to Prague
I went to Anagram just off Týn

And bought Tomaž Šalamun's
*Ballad for Metka Krašovec*

I knew it would be there :
Metka and Tomaž are married
(or were when last I heard)

Then I got drunk on the Jakubská
And the fogs of Praha came over me

All week I slept entirely alone. Even
That may be a slight exaggeration.

*3

Stephen, you are losing yourself

The two cafés you best remember
Rough ones with scratches and benches
(one close by the Kampa, the other off
Konviktská, and both up alleys) are
Shut and being done up for trade.

You've bought two books :
A small edition of Nezval's *Básně Noci*
And something of Giacometti's prose
Just because you wanted to : no
        better reason.

Stephen, you are losing yourself.
The woman who loved you has left you.
Surely you must know that. Go out
Into the wheat fields of Europe
        And sleep.


*4

Frightening this hatred
This passionate un-love for
Someone you still love

Who was the abuser, who the abused ?

Or is it true that both of you still …

Love each other I mean and therefore
Hate the logic of living that has so

Bludgeoned love to death

*5

No. Truth is
That in this city I have destroyed
Whatever I once knew of a woman
Whose existence I had deranged
And whose existence had
Deranged me.


*6

The night of
The Ceremonial Banquet
At the Monasterial Brewery (Strahov Courtyard 302)
I went home early to Mrs. Vorlíčková's
And had cold starters and Budweiser in Na Tetíne
Just before its kitchen closed

Strange isn't it, little one
Those we love the most
Are the ones we end up hating, precisely because
They are the ones we most love

We who aborted each other
In the absolute impatience of our angers
In the intricate tearing of our nerves

*7

I have come to
Praha (Nusle District, tram no. 11)
Seemingly to break down or else to avoid so doing

I have run screaming from the conference
And the best moments have been drinking wine
On the Míšenská just round the edge
From the house of Vladimír Holan

I can't speak any more.
I have long abandoned the science of conversations.
I crave just one day in the Moravian spring.
I look forward to the town of Olomouc, to friends
And sleeping and talking about Ivan Blatný.


*8

The year I disappeared into the Moravian country
Was the best year of my whole and my unwhole life

Those who joined me spoke only of the High Tatra
Those who took me apart managed somehow to put me
together again

*9

In all the time
I was in Praha
I never once walked out to the suburbs
Or took a tram to its end-stop

Little one,
What is it about anger
That drives pain in on its tendered self
Coiling and then slamming prejudice
          into the coma of love ?


*10

No, that is not true.
Each day I jumped the tram to its terminus
To the bistro at Ďáblice, the bus-shelters of Spořilov
Or the proletarian estates of Hůrka

What is it about anger
That drives knowledge away from the brain

What is it about blood
That drives it pulsing to the cunt
Beyond the archive of the eyes

Little one

\*11

In the afternoon heats
I fled both myself and the mid-city traumas
And went up to the eating-house above Trója

Wave on wave of anger pulsed through me

All of the hatreds piling up
Were balanced back by the dark
Garden yard of the immigrant bistro,
The owner who spoke Turkish, Arabic,
Czech, Kurdish, English, Persian
                    at the very least

And the site workers taking time off
To watch Republika Czecha getting through
Their semi-final, smashing Sweden at ice-hockey
In the quietest of all noisiest rooms


\*12

The blue beads
Round your neck, little one
Are what cannot translate time

They are the tiny fish-hooks
That lodged themselves inside me.
In the sea-swirl of the labia and clitoris
They are also flesh of me

*13

These Moravian hills and trees
These horizons of white writing
These church villages and rape fields

This rush of green to the west and the water
This loss of both silence and anger in the harshest
Of all language, in the angers of love …


*14

You millions of trees in the Pardubice meadows
You branches of lilac in the Moravian spring
You bent down women digging early potatoes
You teenage girls fishing carp in mild May ponds
You streams and scarp slopes and spruce stands
You firs and eagle hawks flirting brown wings

*15

What a superb rainstorm
Over the mushroom fields of Bohemia

What an atrocious downpour
Across the lonely railyards of Europe

All the roads become rivers
The rivers become roads

Come little ones, children,
Kurds and you without country or wall

Come and drink from these wet ruts
These generous fountains for the speechless

Or Heaven has come too soon
In these meadows not so far from Terezín


*16

City on the hill
Train rushing west into the bloodshot night
Sky that must be menstruating
Unrequited curve of the delineated earth
River that is a perfect reflection of its skies

When I stroke you
Blood that pulses beyond the archive of your eyes
When I stroke you what coils and then falls back
Is the violence of our breathing

Reach out, little one, touch me

*17

Those last days in Praha
I found some money in a hole in the wall
That was a bitter better stroke of luck

So I went to play pool in the Café Louvre
And then looked for the poetry of silence in
The alleys behind Husova and Na Perštýne

Later I went out to Palmovka on the tram
And stayed drinking in the tenement blocks
Out there & in Na Kotlárce and Na Hájku

Until the dawn tram chairlifted me to Žižkov
And the blood sun rose upon another day

*18

O you matted frescoes of St. Kliment
I was sucked out of this city in thin tubes
I was womb-hoovered of my love

What was left in the airport bin-bags
Was the throbbing artery of time

Little one

# III

## FOR ESMAIL KH'OI

But this poem
　　　　is for you, Esmail,
　　　　　　even though it started
　　　　　　　　out written
　　　　　　'For Mehdi Akhavan
　　　　　　　　Sales'


For part of you is in Mehdi Sales
　　　　　　and part of Mehdi Akhavan is
　　　　　　　　in you :

　　　　a floor of words, a wheat of discourse,
　　　　a meadow of fodder and flowers,
　　　　　　and a
　　　　　　storehouse of
　　　　　　　　　　language …


The face of that Khorasani
　　　　　　sometimes appears in my dreams :
　　　　　　he passes a few words to me
　　　　　　and I have to juggle
　　　　　　　　them :

For words are there to be played with and play
　　　　is a form of laughter and laughter
　　　　　　allows us to breathe
　　　　　　and breath

　　　　　gives birth to the poem

and the poem gives us freedom
                    and freedom allows
                              us to laugh

And, as through your life,
          you take off your tie
                    and your hair gets longer and whiter,
                              so also


You smile more, more live your life in the tree,
          in the poem, in the poem-tree,
          unconcerned with the idiocy of drawn
                    boundaries


And the squirrel of language comes to greet you,
                    comes to your room
                                        as you sleep
                    and, since
you pull yourself in quiet as the poem of the desert,
          it comes to you, the squirrel of
                    laughter & words

While outside night trees rise in waves of withheld
                    sanities ...


          Esmail, these words and this poem
                    are for you :

Translate them back into Persian, or else put
them now into silence which – after
all – is the language
I've made
them
come
from

## ANCIENT SUNLIGHT

I've never driven a car but no-one ever's given me
praise for that

I decided at age eighteen not to take the driver's seat
but to see the city with my feet

I walk to work through a local map of trees, one that
I concocted as I please

I rub local borough workers up wrong ways, double
checking how they plant their trees

I walk to work : as I walk the rhythms of words form
somewhere inside me

Then they well up – as do intuitions – and jerk free :
that also is why I walk to work

Whenever I can I walk on the camber of roads : even
in the congestion of London town

This is possible because great tracts of shining words
glint in the sun & shed shards

Many things are possible in the city : baking bread,
growing vegetables, raising kids

You wouldn't think these things possible & yet they
still are !

I walk along pavements carrying sun-banners made
by wee lads in school yards

I walk along the pavements carrying with me words
spoken by tired schizophrenic old men

I walk along the pavements carrying the burden &
sad retinue of quotidian dementias

And I unfurl those banners of gyres & colour as I
walk across main roads

I furl & unfurl my words : I make poems as I walk
I walk to work with words

My carbon footprint is very low, but my feet have
printed poems throughout these roads

I walk the streets of Whitechapel with the blue bag
of language slung across my breast

I walk the streets of Stepney talking just as I please
but even so only silence rises

I go into pubs and cafés and no-one asks me to sing
I walk to the door & a poem comes in

Ancient sunlight plunges through my veins. What I
know of language is harsh as rock.

Ancient sunlight plunges through my veins from the
constricted depths of dead dockers' docks

Ancient sunlight plunges to the gyp of my stomach
& larded words rise through my gullet

Five thousand years ago a mushroom-gizzarded man
            climbed inside a glacier

Only now – just a few moments back – out he came !
            I walk as his shadow : he is mine

To breathe he staggers through our century drunk
            on ancient sunlight-wine : ancient sunlight

Is how he has given me song, ancient sunlight is
            where poetry & language come from.

## THIRTY-SIX SHORT
## TAKES ON PAIN

*partly after Attila József*


forgive me, dear
heart, but I can't bear this pain :
it hurts too much

*balle, bekh, balle*
sweet one, lamb on the hill
it hurts too much

you gave me your
body above & your body below
but it hurts too much

your mouth on my
mouth my breast on your breast
it hurts too much

this world in my blood and
in my head : too harsh to betray –
but it hurts too much

straight of my back,
body where you died a little :
it hurts too much

skin and you shiver
spilling out over my finger
it hurts too much

sweet-smelling hair
tiny gentian bursting hillside air :
it hurts too much

body in pain
little death that comes again
it hurts too much

body of the tide is breaking
body of the breathing's shaking
it hurts too much

wave on wave on wave until
my measured breaths burst the hill
it hurts too much

when the tremor comes again
along the backbone's ripple span
it hurts too much

when the stunned earth's
ripped apart, closely by my pumping
heart, it hurts too much

little body of my breath
little suckler at your breasts
it hurts too much

forgive me where
the pain is greatest, forgive
the ocean and the foetus

forgive me where
I kill a little, forgive me where
I bite your nipple

forgive me for
the bridge you gave me, when you
arched your back to save me

when I fell
through fire and memory
it hurts too much

and when I get
my strength again, when
I need not fear this pain

when its all that I
can do, to reassert my
sense of you

and when your beauty
and your numbness shatter on
my splintered oneness

when I see you
as you are, standing, falling –
away from me –

breaking jar – then
you're gone and I am broken :
it hurts too much

light of the
world streaming right through you :
it hurts too much –

light of the
world streaming through to me
it hurts too much –

come through this
breakdown and breakdown again
it hurts too much

come through this break
down and break down the pain
it hurts too much

arch your back and
I'll come to you : where
it hurts too much

open your body
and pull me inside you :
it hurts too much

let me stroke you
as the sea-swirl evokes you
it hurts too much

when my body
breaks again, scream in pain
it hurts too much

when the coma
crests curve down : line on line
it hurts too much

to find the world
that we were gifted, in the spilt light
where we left it

then perhaps I'll
realise all the tiny deaths we died
but it hurts too much

now you are gone
and your body says 'no' :
it hurts too much

when all I can
write is the pureness of pain
it hurts too much

the pureness of
pain as it hits me again :
it hurts too much

## HOUSES & FISH : KITE-POEM

I remember their

        names :


    Nabil,                       Shelina

           Billie Blue

   Lindsey,

Nasima,              Lynton,          Habib

     Aktar,

               Sayera

   Raju,
         Michael,


      Julekha,



                  Tara,

    Sadiqua,

       Samantha,

Cashael,

Roxanne,

Abdul,

Daniel,

Abdul,

Samantha,

Bablu,

Gemma,

Abu Anas,

Nicola,

Davina

I remember how they drew

stars and painted houses

And I remember the words

they painted onto their dreams

ordinary words, dream words

:

house, birds, star,

sand, moon, tree, bed,
flower, window

tree, flower, sun, fish

starfish, oldfish, eggfish,
coloured fish,
fish with ears

seaweed-fish, flower-fish

lion, bird, snake & snake's
brother & snake's sister

& snake-fish


I remember how they wrote
the obdurate delights of colour :

blue, red, purple,

bloa, rad, porpol :

I remember that
there were children called
michaelnabil and children
called julekhadavinagemmaabu

and armedeniel

And I remember how stars were painted
with hearts into their dreams

and how houses were faces and
that fish were cars
that could never
crash

that fish were houses and houses
were fish and how

we all of us swam through
the city with its

sky of mango and crushed
brick

and how shoals of tiny-fish coursed
in our blood
and cascaded through our
kidneys

and how plankton
that were cousins, aunts and
enemies fed
in the sluices
of our bellies

And I remember how these
five-year-olds played in
the yards

and how I'd be out there
with them or

how I'd look out from
the staff-room first floor
window

kneeling on the desks
to see the whirling of stars and
fish

and how then we'd painted
a banner full of
summer colours

and then I'd sailed it north from
Wapping to Aldgate

in and out the traffic floes
negotiating calm

against the logic of journal-truth
and government

with bread and history in my
sack, with wet-fish

and rock-salt, with pome-
granate clusters,

with yeast-bursts and blueberry
& memory


I remember their second names :

Mohammad Ali, Hussain,
Barnes,
Begum,

Woodman, Rahman, Miah,
de Farias, Morgan

Hussein, Uddin,
Chambers,

Khan, Corrall, Mason,
Karim, Rahman,

Brown, Rippingale,
Piggott, Mukith,

Choudhury, Hibbard, Uddin,
Steele, Gayle


All of us stars constellated on
the board of the sky :

and where are we now …

and where are we now …

and where, and
where and where

are we now …

## POEM FOR IVAN BLATNÝ

Your body looking
out of your body as a child –
how could it ever have foreseen
the end of your life as
an old man ?

Those photographs
of you standing as a child
self-assured and bone-relaxed
and the images of your parents
free as few mothers or fathers
at that time rarely seemed –
those clear yardages
in white rooms in Brno
or holidaying in spas or
summered at Meudon –
how can they square with
the vitiated hospitals
and sanatoria, Ipswich's
final House Of Hope ?
The white splendour of
Clacton's Endesor, sunlight
spilt along new paths,
Southend's Hotel Weir,
the body unable to call
out for more.

Frances Meacham
met you where you
were at your most
totally forgot. And
after your death thick

volumes of your poetry
were published in Praha
and solemn quartets
played to honour you
and the un-substance
of your memory.

Those photographs of your
last years – that I have copied
from books in great libraries –
break me even to look at you.
The assured stance of pleasure
given over to slumped discharge,
as non a person in asylum hostels here
as you'd been forced to be back there
in soviet socialist denial.

Your father as if you'd never known …
your mother gone in a swirl of dust
as from lost time's white lace …

I think about what happened
to you arriving in London at the plush
of Brunswick Gardens, Cranley Mews,
South Kensington : and within a few years gone to
poverty and neurasthenias on the other side of town :
Toynbee Hall, Stepney streets, Whitechapel Library
where you went to never see your poems.
Rhodedendra, sycamore, sparrows.
Claybury on a whim of crime.

I wonder whether you gave in
to acceptance : feigned illness as
a measure to fetter survival ? By

the time your doctors taught you to know
chlorpromazine, modecate, depixol,
lorazepan : you knew your name too well –
the slump of your body, your face with
all its masks pulled off, your eyes glittered
to nothing. Was that how you learnt to
be : taking survival to be a hidden
alchemy into your dark daze.

Poetry was not a house to be safe in
nor even a place of farce and risk.
The House Of Hope was not a house of hope :
there was not a tree in the railway gardens
was a tulip tree or trunk of heaven
as might trees and gardens have been
in your zones of childhood memory.
Back in Brno where Jiří Orten lived
and died talking to you all the time.
There in Ipswich where Jiří Orten lived
on in your memory as what was real.
Since what was real was not, but a maul
or mewl of tabloid and burnt print
and news entered your mind playfully
and wreaked ordinary pains and joy
such as you could cope and smile to.
A little crease has opened in your mouth.
A place to lie, a little further south and
you might've found somewhere peacefully
to die or to dredge up fathomed air.
A grease-comb to pass before your
eye, a hand to flatten out your hair.
Or your hand to flatten out your
wayward face recumbent in
            its favoured lair.

As you grew older you
shrivelled in your chair : your legs got
longer, your slightly lolling head
told you words to sleep, to go back to bed,
to go to that place from where the face
of all that meant life to you palpably
withdrew and was withdrawn …

As you grew older, your
macaronic script grew open, bolder
uninhibited, unconcerned with what
anyone else might think of such a hand
as could write such palpable un-sense
as should be thrown away or burnt.
It's a pity there is no negative of can't.
Or that you couldn't live within a rent.
Or that neurasthenias beget unlicence
Or that your case was not treated with
A dose of birdsong or tree-bark grease.
You didn't have to live with tax reform.
You never saw the foxes on the green.
Your window whether it opened or not
was open to Rumi or Rilke or Orten to
come climb in and stir about your head
and make of you such prodigious cake.
What dreaming had you when not dead
is what you wrote in multilingual fury :
What calm you had when not so abed
let you know that what's most distant
is the closest to our hearts : what's far
suddenly's what's most near to us here.
Petrol-logic keeps us back from there.
Such phases splashed across your face
as ache in patters of unkempt speech.

Ivan, whatever anyone may say :
a warm embrace – I salute you
& the dereliction of your day.

## BACK FROM RAVENSEAT

One fine, sharp, clear &
lucid, even warm early June-time day
Rev. Tim Tunley drove us up to Ravenseat
and after the little girl of the farm had shown
me all around the yard – her farm, all the sheep
and shovel and dogs, the skipple-heap of it, even
the place her ma said it was ok for wains to wee –
I climbed the stream and set out across the moor
to Tan Hill, a shepherd's path in a shimmer sky,
two rolls and a couple of pints by the black fire
in the highest pub there is in England. Strange.
I was walking roughly east-west, and in the Bar
a Litchfield business-man was stopped with two
Ukrainian guys – that much I could guess from
an angle in their talk and some tad of intuition –
who had hosted him in Kiev and down the Don.
Their long north-south route went from Perth
to the Peak District, roading it out of Appleby,
just now headed for Keld and Muker meadows,
and the barns that are word-hoards on the hills,
then over the rocky tops and edges into Hawes.
All the words we speak are maps for loneliness.
All the sounds we whirl are hope for loveliness.
I left them at Tan Hill and set off on a path over
the moor that soon dwindled and lost itself and
became no path but petered out in bog moss &
sphagnum & mulch & lost-posts & brown juice.
That was a hot post-noon on the tops, near enough
seeing from Lancashire to the North Yorks coast,
from Morecambe Bay near to as far as Cleveland.
And hours later I emerged on the sharp east tips
off Arkengarthdale moor, Faggergill shining in
the silver of its stream, the hamlets of the farther

slopes, barns & huts glinting on a green brocade
like they were night stars shone in still clear day.
Almost, that's all that can be said. Almost I began
talking in a language I no longer knew. Odd, but.
What happened to me on the high tops in the sun?
The tongue no longer in my head but on free air.
Outcrops of shale & lime, little wizen-trees, thick
bogs and black oozes, even birds sparse, tiny wild
flowers, stony basins, no-one seen at all for hours.
Then the broken lead workings, mine of shafts &
tip of tines. Almost, we can make it back to where
we all started from, where fresh memory is torn.
Some Australian choir singing Pergolesi *a capella*
inside St. John's church, outside – a sun of wool.
Dark Black Sheep in the village pub, cream-teas
in back meadows, rivers walking with their trees,
and the great anti-martyrdom of light and shade.
Just us ordinary folk are here for what we made.
Back in the hills industrial ghosts, giants, mock
what we'd have come so far to materially achieve.
A jug of orchids, or five fine hives for honey bees.
Now let these words go wild and crop the hills –
but leave me wandering vacant on high tops until
suddenly I see our tongues were born of silence

# WHAT MIMI SAID TO RUMI

(for Mimi Khalvati)

What Rumi said – in answer to his Shams – is
something only ever
written down in dreams. The frail line between
grace & what's clumsy is but a shining song :
or so it seems


What Mimi heard me say – in answer to her soft
hello – was "on the ropes"
when what I'd mumbled her about my work– that
day we met in the strange café – was "all of it's
on the backs of envelopes"


I wondered where that lilac tree had gone, what
dervish with a tongue
had made it disappear, thinning it beyond thinned
air, to where it had been when it hadn't yet even
been begun.


Our words are shinings, playing with such light,
playthings bathing in
the reek of night, furling eyes out of sad neuroses.
Nothing's lacking if whatever we may suppose
is what our words evoke

What Mimi thought of Rumi was quite clear, not
                    veiled by intervention,
what plaything curved raw meanings through his
air she took delight in, and for her the shining's
                    never ended


What Rumi thought went beyond what I could see
                    into some golden light's
unfrequent frequency that plumed bright yardages
of air, then freed them to the lilac tree so I could
                    see them there !


What Mimi said to Rumi must have been this : how
                    can the shining song not light us up
when all words recede ? What Rumi said in answer
to his Shams is something only ever written down
                    in dreams.

## OLD MAN COMMERCIAL ROAD

The man stood upright by the door
  drinking cans of amber raw

The man stood silent out of time
  drinking jars of bottled wine

The man from far away stood near
  silent so that we might hear

If we want to, if we care, and if we
  don't then he's not there

Every time I pass by there, he has
  his hands around a jar

Every time I'm asking why, if I
  ask him, there's no reply

If I try to talk, his face stays still :
  who am I to think he's ill

Why should he be wrong, not me,
  or me not see his agony

If I think beyond my skin, I begin
  to know where he has been

If I think beyond my shut-eyed eye
  I just begin to fathom why

He's brought his history with his
  skin, where he has been

I can't go in, I cannot begin to see
  what has burnt his memory

But he's not done this to himself :
  little orphan of all wealth

I begin to sense where he might be,
  he might be very close to me

He drinks his beer in jars & cans
  wraps of paper on his hands

What passed across the poet's face
Was the full force of estuarine mud
The total amnesia of a total disgrace
A century of clerk-indentured script
The silences behind a baul's eyelips
The crack of air in a jatra actor's no
A wild smile on the doused ferryman
A year's rain between Barisal & yes
Colour's intensity in an open mango
The flag of thirst on a hunger march
The river swaying between its zeros
All of these and never enough : life
Itself passed across the poet's face

What passed across the poet's face
Was the full force of alluvial dusts
Absolute fiction in an absolute love
Turn of death that won't forget life
The prayer-flag of a sufi's ambition
A netful of boal stowed in the hold
A middleman cut in a bloated belly
A battleship of dalits sent out to die
A thorn-tree in the eyes of ten fish
A harvest of paddy lost to a torrent
The full ferocity of national debris
All of these – but far from enough :
Death itself stormed the poet's eye

What passed across the poet's face
Was enough to fracture all his life
What passed across the poet's face
Was raw beauty in an insane mask
What passed across the poet's face
Was love's grace in all its disgrace
What passed across the poet's face
Was too much for one man to bear
What passed across the poet's face
Was just enough to stop his tongue
What passed across the poet's face
Was life itself in a shattered house
All of this and more than enough :
Life itself stormed the poet's face

## NIGHT SECURITY GUARD, FIELD-
## GATE STREET

"But what are you doing there ?" I said
                              to him,
stood on the scaffolding of the old
        Doss House's first floor,
the clock moving its tight fists round
              way past midnight.

And as answer he gave me the title of my
        poem, even as I said to him :

            "I have to write this poem
about this building, its absolute history,
though no-one has asked me to & no-one
            is paying me for it, & about
the lives of all the people who have ever
              stopped in here"

And saying this, he acknowledged me with
        the gratis of his hand :

So, "therefore" I said "where do I begin ?"

With the moon-faced girl sat by the grating
        of the ground-floor stair way
              past midnight ?

I said nothing, nonetheless she did say 'hello'

With the cats that scurried right through all
        the wee hours of the night …

But they had carried off all the maritime air
that feeds the art of memory

"Where's justice in any of this ?" I said &
he laughed, but he was laughing
with & not at me at all

And the tenement shook with a century of
fiction.

He stood there as if near a café in Kraków.

He stood there as if outside Vaga Bookstore
in Geminidas Ulica in Vilnius.

He stood there as if his life depended on it.

He stood there as if he were wading through
snow, or as if snow were scraping his
scratch cards for him

He stood there as if he were trying to wrap
a condom round a chimney

He stood there as if 'autistic' & 'artistic'
were the same word – which
of course they are

He stood there as if time had never started
in any of the wide streets of Whitechapel
or certainly had never finished

I no longer knew where I had come from
or to where I was going …

But suddenly, walking home, I looked back
and saw the future laid out like a toy
& it gleamed inside my eye

# POEM WITHOUT A WORKING TITLE

I never sang a poem in the Torriano Bar,
    but accompanied by a guitar &
        given good attention …

I never cooked mackerel with ginger for a
    troupe of clowns in Kentish Town.

I never read my poetry at the Festival in the
        ancient town of Stari Grad on Hvar,
    nor for that matter at any festival
        in England either …

I never ran a pub on the western coastline of
    Norway sending the stragglers home
        in the simmer dim.

I did not stand on my balcony in London for
    thirty-five years watching all the wee
        ones grow to their delinquence

I never broke into the homes of my neighbour
    and stole his laptop, his essays on
    Makhmalbaf, his poems on the sufis &
        the nomads

I did not laugh at the desperation of my father
    on the 214 bus, me a three year old girl
        speaking only Mandarin.

I did not disprove Zeno's theorem by drinking
    down every pint I bought against
        the cold dregs of love.

I did not ever think the words 'tired to the bone'
referred more to old men than to children,
but in stubborn joy to one &
all : the same !

Nor did I ever differentiate age, when I was old
or when I was young (& what do these
distinctions mean anyway ?)

I was never raped as a nine year old child in
a children's home. And it is too easy
to say that. Ever.

I did not shout "mother-fucker" after the poet
as he walked away from me up
the street of dreams

I did not let off bombs in buses or banks nor did
I sleep in the hotels of the rich, or porter
with the ghosts of the poor

I did none of these things & yet I lived a full life
balancing time in the lucid days
of my breath

And then the owl of poetry flew across my face
and said to me 'burn all your poems',
'shred all your books'

And I did – and I was happy and I went running
off alone into the deep zones of the pig-herd
of all pain

I went flying into the night-times of the white
owl of all speech, leaving behind me
the clamour of

My fastidious community, a lozenge of hate
in the melt of my reason …

## MEDITATION AT THE WINDOW

The anarchist alleys where Avrom Stencl walked
bright in sunlight dark with sun's battered work
new cobble-stones full with language yet & words.
Alleys where the false historians lurk, their hard-
hats gurgling festivities of sullen centenary grief.

Or the real alleys where Bill Fishman stops to talk.

I think of the friends who've known this angry world :
then see them all walking here fast beneath my eyes.
See them seething : Ivan & Alan, Rachel & Daniele.
Know this planet is a little sphere, this tiny pin-prick
where we look & see our blood-flows pattern stars.

Look ! There's old Ahmed pulling his trolley home.

And as I stand here meditating at the open window
looking over at bare walls and abandoned vaults &
workshops where a year ago my friend hammered tin
I'm also standing wherever else I've been, at windows
looking over stunned and inland seas, at windows
opening onto mountain valleys and cherry orchards
at windows overlooking the churn of urban screams.

And when I stand here meditating with Theo in my
arms, this fifteen months old guy who looks at me &
charms the bird-words out of my branching mouth :
We look and see blue sky or stars or rucksacked men
or corporation carts, gangs of girls or coloured cars,
but say to each other 'look there's fox going home'.
Then we walk, me holding him, he holding me and
making new geometries we venture out to see how
the star-sparkled world is doing in its absence.

We talk and hang on tight in this world where words
prevail and silence is looked askance and meditation's
thought to be some poor alternative to an assault rifle.
We all walk alone, thin as breath or hair, flake or bone
we all walk to the seething stations or finish beneath
mountains that hold snows through heat-raw summer.
But I want to say poetry is a vital art, pumping bright
blood through our heart, poetry is laughter, poetry is
breath. Poetry's a translation out of silence and, for
sure, translation's the opposite of making war.

## MY FRIEND, YOU WHO ...

My friend, you who came
down from the mountains to talk
to me : I have to tell you
                  this –

There is no point in your conversation.
I have passed beyond the laws of the living
beyond language or anthropology or insomnia.
Beyond television or politics or benevolent lies.
Beyond insomnia that is language or politics or
anthropology or television or the benevolence
                            that lies

Do not ask anything of me again.

I will not give it to you. There may be micas or
horneblendes hidden in schists, or human warmth.
Or lepidopteries or magnesium telescopes or bugs.
Or the futilities of simple mathematics, tired bones
and the furtive ambiguities of detailed equivalence.
There might be the pure truths of television, since
how can what we see deceive. Or the leveragings
of virtual realities. Or cynicisms that are become
swerved geographies, or pure economies. Or ...

Whatever. Don't talk to me. Don't even try.

Don't say anything. Any attempt to speak hurts.
Only if you are already dead or in such kingdoms,
turn back like the fish of infinity, and forgive me
any acts of self-malevolence I may be about to …

I am about to commit.

## TO END WITH ...

Mallow leaf soup with foraged herbs

Salad of lime leaves, winter-cress, chickweed

Dead nettle flowers & borage flowers

Banner Street Flats : fennel & oregano

Quakers' Garden : mallow, magwort, lime flowers,
                        elder flower, winter-cress


Cannon Street outside abandoned corporate building :
                        bitter-cress, lavender, rose

Aldersgate : large crop of chickweed, lime flowers, yarrow,
                        plantain leaves, wildrocket, mint

Elderflower fritters, juneberry juice, mugwort tea

Walbrook Street : gingko leaves


Beautiful secret alleyway off Broslehan Street – mallow, lime
        leaves, garlic mustard, fat hen

Yarrow, lavender, rosemary : behind the Suffolk Street flats.

Royal Statistical Society : tansy, herb louise, daisy footsy indexicus
                        (hay ! hay ! the Daisy Man)

Bank of England window box : rosemary, bay

Memorial Garden, Lamb Street : two strawberries.


Nettle, yarrow & lime-leaf burgers, sea lettuce, purslane

Salad of wild rocket, mustard leaves, fat hen, borage & marigold
flowers


To finish with : gingko, rosemary & mint tea

## WHAT KEEPS ME GOING ...

What keeps me going is what's pulling me apart,
   what keeps me going is knowing

What keeps me going is the Sardinian cook being
   in the Arts Café when he could be
      on the dole

What keeps me going is knowing my grandfather
   knew a language spoken only by
      high-hill shepherds

And that – somewhere – students of language are
   working to keep the gai going : all of progress
      reverts back to the tongue

What keeps me going's remembering the Sardinian
   restaurant worker at the ICA who'd motorbike
      it back from London

To Cagliari every few months & that he'd do it to
   keep his sanity, or to lose the very same
      (Max was his name)

What keeps me going is going to keep my heart on
   my shoulders and allow me to weep

What keeps me going is remembering that Hume
   Cronyn is in Toronto & writing wonderful
      city psalms

What keeps me going is what will stop me in the end
   but that'll be a long way off yet !

What keeps me going is knowing that trees still grow
in Corsica, but for how much longer
I'm not sure

What keeps me going are figs warmed for breakfast
in mid-May when there should be
no figs at all

What keeps me going is knowing that a straight line
is a curve & that all curvature
is straight

What keeps me going is the litany of love & explosion
of verve in the light of the void

What keeps me going is knowing that curved space
is what allows a poor man to live & a
poor woman to know

What keeps me going is knowing that curved space
also carries our dust to the remote segments
of the universe

That this universe is curled back to us while forever
moving away & therefore that this universe
knows about the poor

What keeps me going is that I know that two ravens
flying across Loch Broom are not one

And that the hieratic magmas of An Teallach may
collapse but that language will survive

What keeps me going is knowing the stars of the
universe are patterned into our bones
and our blood

And that our corpuscles & bone are patterned in
the moon, or how else would we know

What keeps me going in the face of unknowing is
the face of unknowing

What keeps me going is the raw of your bloods
dancing the dark then pulling me back
to the core of your cunt

What keeps me going is birth, life, sex and death
in roughly that order, or in whichever
you want